CRANSTON
THROUGH TIME

SANDRA MOYER AND
JANET CULLEN RAGNO

AMERICA
THROUGH TIME®
ADDING COLOR TO AMERICAN HISTORY

America Through Time is an imprint of Fonthill Media LLC
www.through-time.com
office@through-time.com

Published by Arcadia Publishing by arrangement with Fonthill Media LLC
For all general information, please contact Arcadia Publishing:
Telephone: 843-853-2070
Fax: 843-853-0044
E-mail: sales@arcadiapublishing.com
For customer service and orders:
Toll-Free 1-888-313-2665

www.arcadiapublishing.com

First published 2019

ISBN 978-1-63500-100-6

Typeset in Mrs Eaves XL Serif Narrow
Printed and bound in England

INTRODUCTION

Cranston has always been a collection of villages, even when it was still part of Roger Williams's Providence. Starting with the founding of Pawtuxet in 1638, as each group of people settled into a new area of what would eventually become Cranston, they named their small community to distinguish it from other neighborhoods. Often the name was derived from an Indian word for the locale or from the family that first settled it.

Since transportation was still primitive, many people spent their daily lives within walking distance of their home and relied on their close neighbors for their economic transactions and their social lives. The center of government was miles away and most people seldom had reason to travel there. If they met a stranger, they would introduce themselves as an inhabitant of Searle's Corner, Knightsville or one of the other villages. In reality, the fact that the inhabitants so closely identified with their village rather than the entire geographic area that would eventually become Cranston actually prevented it from being a town for many years.

By the early 1700s, these villages had decided that they should break away from Providence and start their own municipality. However, they had to first come up with a name for the new town and on that they could not agree. The Indian names of Pawtuxet, Mashapaug, Mashantatuck and Pocasset each had their own following, but no one wanted the new town to have the name associated with a location that wasn't near their own village. After decades of debate, the citizens finally compromised on Lynn, which was a town in Massachusetts from which many settlers had come. However, in 1754, as the bill for the town's incorporation worked its way through the R. I. General Assembly, the name of Lynn was changed to Cranston in order to honor a former governor and his nephew, who was the current Speaker of the House.

Despite now being part of an official town, people's first loyalty remained with their village. Usually it would have a business area with a general store and other companies like blacksmiths, millers and wheelwrights. Small factories and distilleries offered employment and villages would proudly support their local schools and churches. As time went on, the villages competed to be on trolley routes or railroads that offered access to Providence and other cities, making them more popular places to reside. Searle's Corner even changed its name to Oak Lawn, because the developer thought it was a more attractive name for selling houses.

As the years went on, more villages sprang up as the farmlands became housing developments. But these names continued to be the way people described their local community and often named their churches and schools. Thus, we decided to divide this book by village or subdivision name and show the characteristics that make each a unique place to live.

Our pictorial tour of Cranston begins with the colonial seaport of Pawtuxet and the gracious late-nineteenth century homes of Edgewood. We then travel through Auburn, the twentieth-century civic and business center of the city and on to Arlington, once home to a nineteenth-century textile empire and a nationally known brewery.

The journey west continues to Eden Park, an early suburb with its middle-class homes and businesses located within easy distance to trolleys. Then we move on to the newer development of Garden City, built to accommodate the returning World War II soldiers and their young families. We then proceed to Howard, home to the state institutions since the late 1800s. Further west, we pass Meshanticut, another suburban neighborhood made popular by its convenient trolley access. We continue to Dean Estates, settled in the 1950s with more prosperous homes that parallel the wealth of its original owner, John Dean.

Next we proceed to Knightsville and Oak Lawn, which were early farming communities and still retain some of their historic charm. Finally, we end up in Western Cranston, a vast rural area for most of Cranston's history until suburban homes started to replace farms in the last half of the twentieth century. The transformation continues today.

Villages and Subdivisions of Cranston

1

Pawtuxet/Edgewood

Main Street of Pawtuxet: In 1638, the founders of Cranston settled on the north side of the Pawtuxet River near where it empties into Narragansett Bay. Within a decade, another group of families started the town of Warwick just across the river. As the village of Pawtuxet grew into a thriving seaport, it straddled the river that acted as a border. Various bridges were built to connect the two cities and a main street with businesses and stores was developed.

PAWTUXET FISH MARKET: Being right on the waterfront, Pawtuxet was a busy seaport and supplied the area with fresh fish. Originally, the Sam R. Green Fish Market was located at this corner of Bridge and Broad Streets. The market was then owned by J. Steven. The building was heavily damaged by fire in 1892. Next it was operated as Wilbour's Pawtuxet Public Market. Many other businesses have flourished, such as Dear Hearts Ice Cream and Bobby Pins Salon.

WATSON'S PHARMACY: Located at 2206 Broad Street, this Pawtuxet drug store was opened in 1889 by Walter E. Watson in a small end-gable building at the corner of Broad and Bridge Streets. Known as "Doc Watson's," it was the only pharmacy between the Pawtuxet Bridge and Providence. The pharmacy remained in the Watson family ownership until 1972. Ten years later, it became Cameron's Pharmacy. In 2013, a demolition crew took apart the enormous rooftop billboard, a focus of attention for decades. Stores have continued to occupy the building.

TRINITY CHAPEL: The Episcopal parish in Pawtuxet traces its origins to 1883 when a drive to establish a place of worship in Cranston began. Many English workers in the early American textile industry embraced the Episcopal religion over their former Church of England. Trinity Chapel held its early services at 137 Sheldon St. and used that building until the new church was built in 1909 overseeing Stillhouse Cove at 109 Ocean Avenue.

RHODES-ON-THE-PAWTUXET: Thomas Rhodes started a clambake restaurant and dance hall on the shore of the Pawtuxet River in the 1890s. Although the building burned down in 1915, Thomas and his brothers rebuilt it on the same site. Rhodes-on-the-Pawtuxet grew to include boating, canoeing, and bowling. In the 1940s, its Dance Pavilion featured Big Bands led by Glenn Miller and Guy Lombardo. Rhodes-on-the-Pawtuxet remains a popular venue for proms, weddings and meetings of all types.

EDGEWOOD YACHT CLUB: Once a sparsely settled farming village, in the 1870s Edgewood was developed into a suburban enclave for prosperous Providence business owners. Street cars made it easy for them to commute between Providence and this fashionable residential area. Stately homes were built near Narragansett Bay and to accommodate the residents' love of sailing, the Edgewood Yacht Club was built in 1889 and withstood several hurricanes over the years. However, in January 2011, it burnt down to the pilings. The modern version was erected on the same spot and in a similar style.

RI YACHT CLUB: Edgewood is the site of another yacht club a little further south. It was originally named the Providence Yacht Club and was located on Allens Avenue in Providence in 1875. However, by the late 1880s, the name was changed to the Rhode Island Yacht Club and a three-story Victorian clubhouse was erected on Big Rock in Cranston. This clubhouse was washed away during the Hurricane of 1938 and its replacement was destroyed in Hurricane Carol in 1954. But the members were persistent and two years later built a new one-story clubhouse a little further inland near Stillhouse Cove.

NORWOOD AVENUE SCHOOL: The original wooden, four-room school was built in 1892. Sixteen years later, a ten-classroom school was added next door for the older students. In 1954, the older school was closed and eventually was razed and replaced by an apartment building. The larger school building stopped being used as a neighborhood school around 2002, but was retained by the school department for other educational purposes.

EDGEWOOD FIRE DEPARTMENT: Members of the volunteer fire company in this *circa* 1920 image are seen with their 1911 truck. Before 1850, no city in the United States had paid full-time firefighters, and volunteer firefighters played an invaluable role in protecting lives and property. Benjamin Franklin believed that a volunteer firefighter will work harder and longer than any paid firefighter because they chose to be there. Currently, Cranston has five fire stations and no longer uses volunteers. This station on 131 Park Avenue serves the Edgewood area.

ROGER WILLIAMS MAUSOLEUM: Thomas Cullinan opened this private mausoleum abutting Roger Williams Park in 1926. It was erected as a beautiful three-story granite building with a stained-glass window over a marble altar which serves as a memorial to veterans of American wars. When the last heir died in 2002, no money was left for maintenance of the building. It was condemned and would require millions of dollars to repair. Close to 500 bodies are still interred there.

2

AUBURN

BRIGGS SCHOOL: This building was built in 1904 as Cranston's new high school. However, when the demand for secondary education grew, a new high school was built in 1925 near the original building. The older school became Briggs Junior High School, named after William Briggs, who was the superintendent of school for nine years. After Park View Junior High opened in 1954, the Briggs building became the site of school administration offices. However, when the neighboring building became overcrowded in the 1990s, the top two floors of the Briggs building once more were used for classrooms.

CRANSTON HIGH SCHOOL: The larger high school was built in 1925 on the other side of City Hall from Briggs. Over the years, the school has been enlarged many times, adding a more modern gym, cafeteria, science labs and classrooms. When the population of the western side of Cranston surged, a second high school was built off Phenix Avenue in the 1960s. The new school was named Cranston High School West and the original high school added East to its name.

ROLFE SQUARE: With the city hall, high school and junior high occupying the space on the corner of Park and Pontiac Avenues, the area became the civic center of Cranston. A small triangular parcel of land near these buildings became the Memorial Monument Square and three Civil War cannons purchased by Governor William Sprague IV were placed there. Years later, the area was not considered safe for such valuable cannons and they were replaced by weapons from World War II.

BROWN DAIRY: Beginning in 1914, this dairy served the people of Cranston and beyond. Its brown and white trucks were a familiar sight on the roads in the days when practically everyone had milk and other dairy products delivered to their doorstep. For many years, their headquarters were on Park Avenue, right next to Cranston East. The family eventually sold their operation to Hood Dairy and the site was redeveloped as a strip mall with several small stores and businesses.

Dolan Drugs on Park Avenue: Brothers John and Martin Dolan ran a drug store at 734 Park Avenue around 1903. Because pharmacists often made flavors to mask the taste of bitter drugs, they turned this skill into running soda fountains. Dolan's marble fountain served sodas made to order. They also sold cigars, tobacco, medicines and, for a short time, served as the local post office. The Dolan Variety Store sold many items for the home from phonographs to paints and hardware. The building remains recognizable and houses the Ocean Flame Asian Food restaurant.

McGUIGAN'S STORE: This store located at 711 Park Avenue was a popular dry goods and accessories shop from 1894 to 1925. The building and its surroundings were greatly damaged in the Great Hurricane of September 1938, one of the most powerful and destructive storms ever to hit Southern New England. Between 400 and 800 people died that day. Over the years, the building has had many occupants including the Grain Coast Fellowship Church.

STORES ON PARK AVENUE: This street which connects east and west Cranston was a busy commercial center since the 1800s. When the new highway was built, later to be called Route 10, many of the businesses were demolished. The section of the highway from Olneyville south to Reservoir Avenue was built partially along Huntington Avenue and opened in 1960. When the Route 6-10 Connector opened in 1972 and eventually connected to Interstate 95 in downtown Providence, the traffic going below the overpass greatly increased.

LADD HOUSE: Before businesses took over most of Park Avenue, there were some stately houses situated there. This house owned by the Ladd family is one such example. The three-story house was built in 1865 and had sixteen rooms. It was torn down in 1948 and several stores were built on its site. One of the most popular was a branch of Benny's, the local merchandising icon started by Benjamin Bromberg as an auto store in 1924. It grew to include everything from hardware and clothes to sporting goods and toys. Sadly, the chain closed in 2017.

AUBURN LIBRARY: The Auburn Public Library was established in 1888 as the first library in Cranston. It occupied a small store on the northeastern corner of Wellington Avenue with less than 1,000 books. In 1937, the library moved to a house on 687 Park Avenue and remained there until 1968 when it relocated to a storefront on Rolfe Square. Altogether, the Auburn Library had six temporary homes before a new building, designed specifically to be a library, was built at 396 Pontiac Avenue in 1991. [*Two top photos courtesy of Cranston Public Libraries*]

St. Matthew Church: With the arrival of many Irish and Italian immigrants, the Catholic population of Cranston grew. Churches were built in the newly formed suburbs. Located on the corner of Elmwood and Park Avenues, St. Matthew was consecrated in 1909. Over the next 100 years, the church added a school and a convent. The much enlarged church remains as a strong parish, although the school and convent have been put to other uses.

LINDY'S RESTAURANT: The busy corner of Reservoir and Park Avenues has always been a popular place for businesses that catered to travelers. In the 1800s, the Sandy Fenner Hotel was a stop for stagecoaches on what was then the intersection of New London Turnpike and Knightsville Road. It was demolished in 1934, and in its place, John and Jean DiBona established Lindy's Restaurant, which featured a counter and booths. After attracting crowds for over thirty years, the DiBonas sold the site to the Gulf Oil Company for a gas station. Other gas stations followed and Cumberland Farms occupies the corner.

UNIVERSAL WINDING COMPANY: The large brick complex at 1655 Elmwood Avenue started as a factory for making Maxwell Automobiles in 1908. Six years later it housed what became the world's largest company to make winding machinery for textiles and electric cords. During the two world wars, the company switched to manufacturing military supplies like grenades, machine guns and parachutes. In 1959, it changed its name to Lessona and then moved to Warwick a few years later. Other companies such as Scott Brass have occupied the buildings since.

3

ARLINGTON

GOVERNOR SPRAGUE MANSION: As seen in the *circa* 1950 photo, this two-and-a-half-story mansion has stood at the corner of Cranston Street and Dyer Avenue since the oldest portion was built in 1790. Added on over the years in 1808 and 1864, the house now has twenty-eight rooms. It was the birthplace of two RI Governors named William Sprague who later became U.S. Senators. The family was the largest textile manufacturer in the country during the mid-1800s. The mansion has been little changed and is the headquarters for the Cranston Historical Society.

Cranston Print Works: William Sprague converted the grist mill on his farm into a mill for spinning cotton thread in 1808. After it burned in 1813, he rebuilt it in stone and added machinery for weaving cloth. William and his two sons and three grandsons continued to enlarge the company until by the 1860s, A & W Sprague Print Works was part of the biggest textile empire in the country. When the Spragues went bankrupt in 1873, the company was run by the Knights and eventually the Rockefellers and it was renamed the Cranston Print Works. The site was sold in 2019 to a Massachusetts developer.

SPRAGUE BOARDING HOUSE: Many of the people who worked in the Print Works were immigrants from Ireland. If a worker was unmarried, they could live in a company boarding house that had many small rooms. Those married with families would be housed in the numerous duplex mill houses along Dyer Avenue and the adjoining streets. In the 1950s, the boarding house on Dyer Avenue was torn down and in its place St. Ann's School was built. The school building is now owned by the Providence diocese as a youth center that sponsors a haunted house attraction near Halloween.

Cranston Street Trolley: Originally known as Bull Town, this corner near the Sprague Mansion contained the homes of the English supervisors who oversaw the mostly Irish workers of the Print Works. The name came from John Bull, the popular nickname for Brits. The Spragues started a horse-drawn street car system that connected their property with Providence. By the 1940s, the trolleys ran by electricity. The corner remains a busy intersection.

THE BRICK STORE: The Sprague family not only supplied housing, a school and church for its workers, they also built a store across from the Sprague Mansion in 1858. The mill workers could buy on credit until the end of the month when they would use their wages of around $20 to pay off their debt. Before the store was torn down in 1962, it was used as a library and a YMCA. The strip of small stores that replaced it still caters to neighborhood needs.

DYER AVENUE RAILROAD CROSSING: Since William Sprague controlled the Hartford, Providence and Fishkill Railroad, he made sure that tracks went right to his family's textile mill, making it convenient for them to bring in raw materials and ship out the finished cloth. The tracks went by the cluster of duplex mill houses on Dyer Avenue that they had built for their workers. Many years later, the railroad was gone and these tracks became part of the nineteen-mile Washington Secondary Bike Path that goes from Cranston to western Coventry.

NARRAGANSETT PARK: Amasa Sprague (1845-1919) loved raising and racing horses. He built the large carriage house and stables on the Sprague Mansion property. A little further east, he constructed the Narragansett Trotting Park for horse races. When it opened in 1867, Cornelius Vanderbilt and J. P. Morgan were in attendance. The park later was the site of automobile and motorcycle races as well as civic events. The 1904 photo shows the park's celebration of the Cranston's 150th anniversary. The same land eventually housed Cranston Stadium and Stubbins Field, the site of many athletic events.

NARRAGANSETT BREWERY: Another large company that began in Arlington was a brewery built by German immigrants. Beginning in 1890, the property included a barn, stable and blacksmith forge to take care of the horses that transported the ingredients and the finished beer. Then in 1914, the company added a large bottling plant. The brewery produced the best-selling beer in New England and used the advertising slogan of "Hi Neighbor, have a 'Gansett." After the brewery closed in 1981, the buildings were torn down. A large shopping area of mostly big-box stores was later built.

Arlington Hay, Straw and Feed Store: This business was located at 5 Depot Ave. Once part of the Sayles Finishing Plant, which produced a series of major innovations in the finishing of textile goods, it became a victim of the array of problems that virtually wiped out the entire New England textile industry. It was finally closed in July 1971. Arlington Farm and Pet Supply Company now occupies the building.

DYER MANSION: Charles Dyer built a stone end house on this site in 1732. Later additions were added by his descendants. At first the farm was noted for its cabbages and the area was known as Cabbage Neck, but around 1828, the family planted mulberry trees to feed silkworms. This enterprise was not successful, but they continued to grow ornamental and fruit trees. Many members of the Dyer Family are buried in their family plot on their former farm which became the Pocasset Cemetery. The house no longer exists.

FIRE AT 1051 CRANSTON STREET: Elisha Durfee's auction emporium opened in 1897. This huge building could seat 325 people for auctions of livestock, horses and carriages of all kinds. At 2 a.m. in April of 1905, a fire broke out. Four different volunteer fire companies responded but the fire was so hot that five buildings belonging to Durfee and his brother were burnt to the ground. A shoe containing a human foot was found in the remains. Apparently, someone had sought shelter and started the fire while smoking. Durfee never reconstructed his emporium and the land was rebuilt with houses.

PARK AVENUE: This well-traveled road connecting eastern and western Cranston was once known as Knightsville Road. After Roger Williams Park was created, the road changed to its present name. In the 1920s photo, early cars faced large potholes in the poorly paved street. The newly built John W. Horton School can be seen to the left and the fence on the other side of the road encircles the Narragansett Park. Horton ceased being a neighborhood school around 2002, but the school department continued to use it for special programs.

4

Eden Park/Garden City

Phillips Memorial Baptist Church: Once the trolley lines went into Eden Park, this area became attractive as a suburb within easy reach of Providence. James Budlong wanted to develop part of his farm into house lots. He donated land for a church and in 1901, the original Phillips Memorial Baptist Church was built just east of the Eden Park School, which is also in the photo. In 1956, the congregation built a large brick colonial revival building and now uses the older building as a daycare and church hall.

EDEN PARK SCHOOL: Starting in 1897 and continuing for fifty-five years, the wooden building educated the students of the Eden Park area. By 1920, the population of the area had grown so much that an addition was constructed, giving this Pontiac Avenue school twenty classrooms. In 1952, it was replaced with the one level, brick structure on Oakland Street that also bears the name Eden Park School.

RR CROSSING AT PONTIAC AVENUE: The Pawtuxet Valley Railroad leased their lines to the New York, Providence and Boston Railroad in 1884. The New York, New Haven and Hartford then took over the lines in New England. Beginning in the 1890s, New York banker, J. P. Morgan, attempted to monopolize New England transportation by arranging the New Haven's acquisition of fifty companies. By 1912, the New Haven practically monopolized rail traffic from Boston to New York City. The tracks, still seen in the top photo, were later removed and some were converted to walking/biking trails, others to open space.

Budlong House: This large, twelve-room house is located at 604 Pontiac Avenue. It is one of a several houses that the Budlong family built for family members alongside other lots that they sold to others. The land had been part of their large 480-acre farm that had at one time produced vegetables for the Boston and New York markets. They also were well known for their pickles and roses. Many immigrants from Sweden settled in the area to work on the farm in the mid-1800s. The house remains a private residence and looks much like it did a century ago.

EMERY PARK: In the late 1890s, Orville Leach established Emery Park and Picnic Grounds as a rural recreational area just north of Blackmore Pond. It boasted of the "miraculous" Ponce De Leon Spring with luminous water. Later, a casino and a 125-seat dining hall were built and, when electric lights were added in 1906, nighttime dancing and athletic events took place. Many groups rented the grounds for their outings, including the Cranston Volunteer Fire Co. The Park closed in 1921 and first Bickford's Family Restaurant and then the RI Credit Union were built on the site.

STONE HOUSE: One of Cranston's early settlers, Hugh Stone, a blacksmith, was born about 1638 in England and came to RI around 1657. He moved to the Doctor Aldrich Farm at 1240 Pontiac Avenue where he died in 1728. On this farm was the "Old Stone burying ground," which was removed to the North Burial Ground in Providence where the Hugh Stone Memorial can be found and where his family is buried. The cemetery was moved in order to build the Route 37W off-ramp to Pontiac Avenue.

SHOPPING CENTER SIGN: Garden City was developed by Nazarene Melocarro in 1948 to provide housing for the returning WWII soldiers who were starting families. Streets named after flowers were filled with small ranches and capes. Melocarro provided a shopping center that was in walking distance of the homes. The earliest stores and businesses were locally owned and catered to people's everyday needs such as food, hardware, gasoline and baked goods. Seventy years later, the Garden City shopping area has expanded to over seventy businesses and is a destination shopping spot for people wanting to buy from nationally known stores.

GARDEN CITY MINE: For some time after Garden City was developed, the abandoned graphite and coal mine located next to Reservoir Avenue still remained. It had been started by the Harris family, who, beginning in 1638, owned much of what is central Cranston. After many years of several owners and unimpressive production, the 100-year-old mine was torn down. However, the mine shafts remain under the area and at times portions of macadamized parking lots have become sink holes. This area has become the site of several new restaurants. [*Top photo courtesy of Garden City Center*]

ALMACS SUPERMARKET: Once part of a popular RI chain of stores, Almacs was an early tenant of Garden City. It was located right at the north entrance of Garden City. In the years that followed, the grocery store kept moving to three other Garden City locations with bigger and bigger stores. At one time, it was where the gazebo was later built. Then it moved to the furthest southern end of the shopping center and finally it occupied a building on Sockanosset Crossroads. The chain then went out of business and the original space is occupied by Talbot's. [*Top photo courtesy of Garden City Center*]

GARDEN CITY PHARMACY: Every village needed a drugstore and before big national chains provided every possible medicine, beauty product and health aid, most of these drugstores were family-owned businesses. This pharmacy, owned by the Wiesel family, was located across the street from Almacs. The building has housed numerous service and retail businesses in the years that followed, and Garden City still decorates for the holiday season. [*Top photo courtesy of Garden City Center*]

OUTLET DEPARTMENT STORE: In time, Garden City expanded beyond the section which became known as the Village, and bigger stores were built in the area near Sockanosset Crossroads, named the Commons. Retail department stores such as Outlet, Gladdings and Kennedy's made it unnecessary for people to go to downtown Providence to shop for the latest fashions. Those stores eventually went bankrupt, but the area continues to attract nationally known stores. [*Top photo courtesy of Garden City Center*]

GARDEN CITY CINEMA: In the 1970s, a newer owner of Garden City decided to add entertainment facilities to the development. A bowling alley and a cinema were built on the northern side of Sockanosett Crossroads. Adults and children patronized the lobby and refreshment stand in the cinema. Unfortunately, still another subsequent owner of Garden City believed that these activities were not upscale enough and the area was developed for big-box stores and office buildings.

5

PETTACONSETT

PLANE CRASH OFF PONTIAC AVENUE: Herman Burlingame III learned to fly in open, two-seater planes by taking off and landing in a small airfield in what is now Garden City. In 1940, he crashed his small plane in the meadow behind his grandmother's house at 1077 Pontiac Avenue, capturing the attention of his neighbors. Herman survived this crash but later died, along with his wife, baby and cousin, when a plane he was flying crashed in Ohio after the war. The site of his grandmother's house is now an apartment building.

FRANKLIN/ HOWARD/ PETTACONSETT SCHOOL: Howard was a quiet farming village up until the mid-1800s. This four-room neighborhood school was built in 1888 and used for many years. It was known by several names, including Franklin and Howard Schools. Just before it ceased being used by the school department around 1977, it was known as the Pettaconsett School. The building then became a daycare center before it was used by other businesses.

STATE INSTITUTIONS AT HOWARD: Prior to the late 1800s, Cranston, like most RI towns, operated poor farms to take care of the disabled and destitute in their own communities. Around the time of the Civil War, the idea of the state providing for the care of all the people who needed social services gained acceptance. Two adjacent farms, owned by Thomas Brayton and William Howard, were purchased, and the state began to erect buildings to house Rhode Island's poor, insane and criminal citizens, including the Alms House. Rhode Island still uses the property.

PRISON: A prison, like the Alms House on the previous page, seems like a strange building to promote on a post card, but the state was proud of its then-modern building that housed the county jail as well as the state prison. The pastoral setting was thought to help in the inmates' rehabilitation. The original prison has been replaced by seven more secure buildings, five for men and two for females, and has been renamed the Adult Correctional Institutions (ACI).

SOCKANOSSET SCHOOL FOR BOYS: In 1881, the state added a reform school for boys on the grounds of the state institutions. The school was seen as a rural place where wayward boys could be kept away from the temptation of the city and "reformed" into useful citizens. Besides working on the large farm, the boys were taught trades and encouraged to participate in activities like a marching band. They lived in three-story stone cottages. The school closed in 1985 and twenty-three years later, a few of the cottages were incorporated in the mixed development of businesses, condos and offices known as Chapel View.

CHAPEL: Religion was part of the effort to rehabilitate the Sockanosset School's young inmates. A stone chapel was built in 1891 on the grounds. The attractive stone building featured stained-glass windows and a steeple. Part of the building was used as an infirmary until it burned down in 1970. Around 2008, the chapel was renovated into a fashionable restaurant named Chapel Grille. The main dining room was built in the same space as the infirmary. [*Bottom photo courtesy of the Carpionato Group*]

Oaklawn School for Girls: Located across Reservoir Avenue from the Sockanosset Boys' School and built around the same time, this school housed young females who were deemed wayward. Their offense might be loving a boy their parents disapproved of or not conforming to their role as young ladies. They were taught homemaking skills and usually were employed as maids when they came of age. Brayton Park replaced this place of forced labor with a recreation area that often accommodates female athletes.

PUMPING STATION: By the 1860s, the nearby city of Providence needed a new source of water for its growing population. Cranston provided the solution. The Pawtuxet River was dammed, and a huge pumping station was erected in the village of Pettaconsett to raise the water sufficiently so that it would flow downward to its Providence customers. The station handled five-million gallons of water daily. Ironically, the site of this pumping station for clean water became the location of the WPCF sanitation plant for wastewater.

7

Meshanticut/Dean Estates

House on Sockanosset Hill: Sockanosset Hill was named for Soconoco, a Narrgansett Indian chief who thought that the hill located in what is now central Cranston provided good protection since approaching enemies could be seen. Years later, the land was sold as part of the Meshanticut Purchase of 1662. By the early 1800s, a few families of color were living on the hill. Tilly Garrison and her adopted daughter occupied this house where a shocking crime occurred. The daughter was murdered by her jealous husband. Later, starting in the 1940s, Sockanosset was the site of several housing subdivisions called Colonial Homes, Woodridge and Dean Estates.

SOCKANOSSET RESERVOIR: In 1868, a reservoir was built on the top of Sockanosset Hill to store the water that was pumped up from the Pawtuxet River in Howard. The reservoir covered 14 acres just west of the state institutions that were built around the same time. Pipes were laid to connect the reservoir to Providence and Reservoir Avenue was constructed along the straight right of way. This reservoir closed in 1926 when the much larger Scituate Reservoir was opened. For a while the site was used as a pistol range for the police. In the 1970s, several condo buildings were built there, including West Bel Air.

CORNELL FARM ON PHENIX AVENUE: In the latter part of the nineteenth century, the family of Mason Cornell owned this farm. His descendants prospered as dairy farmers on this land. Years later in the 1960s, the land was sold to the city of Cranston and both Cranston High School West and later Western Hills Junior High School were built here. The farmhouse was on what is now the tennis courts and only a family mausoleum remains of the family farm.

MESHANTICUT PARK: John Dean, a wealthy furniture manufacturer, started a new residential development on his land near Cranston Street in the 1890s. The subdivision appealed to people who wanted the convenience of living near a train station for easy access to Providence and points beyond. To make the area even more attractive, Dean donated 20 acres for a wooded park surrounding a manmade lake. Picnic facilities and a cabin for ice skaters offered yearlong recreation. Today the facilities are gone, but the lake still attracts walkers and skaters.

JOHN DEAN HOUSE: In the early stages of his career, John Dean lived in two large houses on Oaklawn Avenue. When he was at the peak of his wealth in 1904, he built a beautiful twenty-room mansion at the top of Sockanosset Hill in the middle of his apple orchards. He named his estate Tupelo Hill after a rare tree that was located there. Unfortunately, the residence burned down in 1934. All that remains is the carriage house, which is now used as a residence. This area of Dean Estates has many streets named after the apples he grew.

ICE HOUSE: Back in the days before electrical refrigerators, people used ice to keep their food cool. Ice was delivered to a customer's kitchen during the warm months and placed in a wooden box with the food. Supplying this ice was a big business. The ice would be cut from lakes and ponds during the winter, and then stored in large buildings packed with straw. Henry Angell built such an ice house on Angell Pond around 1905. The building is gone and the pond has reverted back to nature.

6

KNIGHTSVILLE/THORNTON

THOMAS FENNER HOUSE: Shortly after western Cranston began attracting settlers, the King Phillip's War between the Indians and settlers broke out in 1675. Many of the settlers' homes were burned and they had to start all over again after the war. This homestead was built in 1677 by Arthur Fenner for his son, Thomas, to live in. Later it was used as a tavern. The building is the oldest in Cranston and is owned by a descendant of the Fenner family who restored the building for use as a bed and breakfast.

Knightsville Meeting House: Baptists in Cranston held a lottery to raise $2,500 to build a new church and, in 1806, they erected this building on Phenix Avenue. When Cranston decided to stop holding their town meetings in rowdy taverns, they were held here for about fifty years. The Baptists sold the church in 1860 and it was then used by the Congregationalists. For many years it was the oldest public building in Cranston until it was torn down around 2015. The replacement building has the same footprint and was built to look like the original.

TOWN HALL: After holding their town meetings in a series of taverns, stores and churches, in 1886 Cranston finally built a town hall at the crossroads of Cranston Street and Park and Phenix Avenues. By the time of this *circa* 1950 photo, the police were using the second floor as their station and the public works building was nearby. Later, the city hall moved to Auburn and the police department moved to a new building. Eventually the old town hall was knocked down. A public park, with a gazebo for concerts, was put in its place.

CRANSTON STREET LIBRARY: In 1926, the Knightsville Library Association was organized, and their first library opened the next year. For thirty years, the library moved to various locations along Cranston Street. Then, in 1957, land was donated and a new library building was established at 1847 Cranston Street. The Association worked hard to raise funds for the building and its contents. In the late1960s, Knightsville Library joined the newly formed Cranston Public Library system. *[Top photo courtesy of Cranston Public Libraries]*

Knightsville School: This school, located on Greene Street, was built in the 1920s when wood was still the primary building material for elementary schools. In 1960, the school was closed, and the students were moved to a new one-story brick building on nearby Mayfield Street. Originally the new school was called West View, but in 1979 it was renamed to honor a neighborhood man, George J. Peters, a paratrooper who had been killed in Germany in 1945 during WWII. He received the Congressional Medal of Honor.

Pocasset Fire Hall: In 1895, a group of Knightsville men formed the Pocasset Hose Company, a volunteer group to protect their area from fire. Two years later they erected the building on Cranston Street as seen in this *circa* 1909 photo. The fire station had a second floor which was used for events such as dances, meetings, and graduations. A group of musicians was formed to accompany the fire company during musters. Since 1924, when the fire company moved further south in the village, the building has been used as a factory and food market as well as a jewelry store.

8

OAK LAWN

EDWIN SEARLE HOUSE: Located at 109 Wilbur Avenue in Oak Lawn, this house was built in 1677 on the site of Searle's previous home that had been burned down in the King Phillip's War. This stone-ender was a small, one-and-a-half-story gable-roofed house, but a two-story addition was added by 1727. It was the Searle family who gave their name to Searle's Corner which was what Oak Lawn was called before 1872. The house has been lovingly maintained over the years and is still used as a private home. A portion of the stone chimney can be seen on the west side.

THOMAS BRAYTON HOUSE: Located at 271 Wilbur Avenue, this one-and-a-half story, five-room, central chimney house with a gambrel roof was built for Thomas Brayton around 1767. The property includes a long, low shed of pegged construction between the house and an early twentieth-century shingled cross-gabled barn. The Braytons were an important family in Oak Lawn, and nearby Brayton Avenue was named after them. The house, which sits at Wilbur Corners near the intersection of Natick and Wilbur Roads, was later purchased by William Mason.

THOMAS BAKER HOUSE: In 1790, Thomas Baker lived in this house at 684 Natick Avenue. It was also owned at times by the Sheldon, Wood, Rathbun, Benauder and Moreau families. Judy Benauder is pictured in the top photo taken around 1938. There was once a mill behind the property and mill stones were used to create the steps in front. There were cemeteries located behind the home and many artifacts from the former mill have been found on the property.

OAK LAWN GRANGE: Before this grange was built in 1914, members held their meetings in their homes. Once the new building was erected, it became the cultural meeting place of Oak Lawn. Barn dances and social events were held for the neighborhood, but its most important function was to cater to farmers with agricultural exhibits and lectures. The grange is still in use as a popular meeting place for local residents.

OAK LAWN LIBRARY: After being used as a school from 1838 to 1895, this small, white, wood-frame building became the home of the village's library the next year. It is on Wilbur Avenue, which was part of the parade route for the village's annual Fourth of July parade held over fifty years ago. In the years since, the library has had additions built in 1965 and 1990. It is now one of the six branches of the Cranston Public Library and serves the growing population of western Cranston.

CALLERY'S STORE: At the corner of Oak Lawn and Brayton Avenues not far from a trolley stop, there was a small house lived in by the Callery family. They ran a small variety store that included smoking materials and a candy counter. The family lived on the second level where they could watch for any customers. Originally the property contained a blacksmith shop, but as automobiles became more popular, the family added a gasoline pump. Since the gas station seen below also offers convenience items, the site's function hasn't changed that much over time.

STAGECOACH STOP: In 1817, a private toll road was built connecting Providence to New London, Connecticut. Horse driven stagecoaches could only go about 15 miles an hour, so taverns would be built along the route so that travelers could stop for meals and overnight lodgings. The Gordon Arnold Stand was built on New London Turnpike. It remained in use as a popular stopping spot even when cars replaced stagecoaches, but it was eventually knocked down. First Meshanticut Green and then 99 Restaurant occupied this location and kept up the tradition of feeding people.

Searle Store at 5 Exchange Street: In 1854, F. S. Turner brought the railroad to what was then Searle's Corner in an attempt to sell the housing lots he had platted from his farm. He also renamed the village as Oak Lawn, which he thought was a more attractive name. Crawford Williams built this store on Exchange Street with a flat roof and a "boom town" front, resembling an old Western town building. The post office was moved to that location then owned by Edwin Searle. It has been the location of various businesses and is now a private residence.

9

Northwest Cranston

BURTON HOUSE: One of the oldest houses in Cranston was built by John Burton in 1743 on what eventually became Comstock Parkway. The top photo shows what the house looked like around 1920 when it was still a farm. About ten years later, when the area was made into a golf course, the building became the clubhouse and dining room for its members. The house, over two-hundred and seventy years old, is once more a private residence.

COMSTOCK GOLF COURSE: Hattie Comstock and her son, Jonathan, were the creators of the golf course that for many years carried their name. Starting in 1929 as a nine-hole course, it expanded to eighteen holes three years later. However, during World War II, the land was once more turned into a farm and leased to tenant farmers to grow food for the war effort. When the war was over, most of the old golf course became a subdivision of homes that was named Comstock Gardens. However, some of the land is still used for farming.

JOY HOMESTEAD: Around 1770, Job Joy built this house on what is now Scituate Avenue. Besides being a farmer, Joy was also a shoemaker. His son, Samuel, expanded both the farm and his skills to include other trades that produced leather goods. In this 1959 photo, the members of the Cranston Historical Society are rehabilitating the house that they had just purchased for their headquarters. The Society still owns the house and uses it for their educational school program that teaches children colonial home activities such as fireplace cooking and spinning.

DUGAWAY MILL: Samuel Joy owned the mill across the road from his house. At first used as a grist and saw mill, over the years the mill had many owners and produced everything from cloth to pickles to energy drinks. The area attracted other artisans and became known as Joy Town, an early industrial site in Cranston. By the 1940s, the mill had fallen into disrepair. It was demolished around 1950 and the land became the Boy Scouts' Champlin Reservation.

Sheldon House: The Sheldon family was one of the largest landowners in early Cranston. Their 3,000-acre farm included five houses for various members of the family. This gambrel roofed cape house at 458 Scituate Avenue is the oldest and was probably built in 1728 and enlarged in 1764. For over 100 years, it was owned by Sheldons. Later owners included the Gladdings family that owned the Providence department store of the same name. The home has been well maintained and is an excellent example of an eighteenth-century farmhouse.

CALEB ARNOLD TAVERN: When Cranston incorporated as a town separate from Providence in 1754, the first town meeting was held in this tavern at 227 Phenix Avenue. By the time of this *circa* 1920s photo, the building had seen better days. The old tavern was torn down in 1946 and a new brick residence was built on the site. As the road became more commercial, the building was used for businesses.

10

SOUTHWEST CRANSTON

HEROD MILL: Not long after the western portion of what was to become Cranston was purchased from the Indians, John Herod, one of the original settlers, started a mill in 1662 using the waterpower from the falls on a nearby brook. He dyed cloth there as well as had a smithy and a furnace, the latter which lent its name to Furnace Hill Brook. Over the years, the mill was used for other types of manufacturing including stoves, braid, dishes and pewter ware before it fell into disrepair in the first half of the twentieth century. The site doesn't look much different now.

FURNACE HILL BROOK: Furnace Hill Brook cuts through a large swath of western Cranston all the way from Plainfield Pike to Route 95 in Oak Lawn. For many years this area had a rural character and attracted many sightseers such as the girls in this *circa* 1925 photo. In recent years, western Cranston has had many residential subdivisions carved out of the woodlands and even solar industrial use has started to mar the scenery. But the same area as where the girls were located remains so heavily wooded that the brook is hard to see.

BRIGGS FARM: The original owner of this land at 300 Hope Road was Caleb Burlingame. He was a direct descendant of Thomas and Elizabeth Burlingame who were the first of the Burlingame family to settle in RI from England. The Caleb Burlingame family cemetery is located behind the school. The house was sold by Stephen Burlingame to the Greene family, then to Frank Briggs who farmed there until he sold the land to the City of Cranston in order to build Hope Highlands Elementary School. In 2017, the elementary school was converted to a middle school.

CORNELL FARM ON BURLINGAME ROAD: At the turn of the twentieth century, Fred Andrews owned the farm on Burlingame Road, pictured above. In 1938, Fred sold the farm to the Cornell family, who also owned a farm on Phenix Avenue. Everett Cornell and his sons ran the successful dairy farm until the 1960s, either selling their milk products and eggs at their dairy stand or through door to door delivery. Eventually, it became the site of the Cranston Country Club.

FLOODED FARMHOUSE: The house at 1410 Hope Road was built as a two-room home before 1700. George Gould, a member of the local Anti-Slavery Association, lived there in 1835. In 1889, George Yeaw and his family were living there when the dam on the reservoir north of his property burst, flooding the farm and the nearby area all the way to Main Street in Fiskeville. Throughout the years, this farm has been a cattle farm, a slaughterhouse, a dairy farm and a horse boarding farm. [*Top photo courtesy of Betty Thurne*]

House Moved to Seven Mile Road: It was very common in the past to move older buildings as they sat on stone foundations and could be easily lifted. In 1947, a building was removed from the Hope Road farm of Kitty Mauran by jacking it up and placing large beams below it. The building was then slid onto a trailer and brought the distance to its future location on Seven Mile Road where a new foundation awaited it. The neighbors had come out to see the house carefully being maneuvered down the streets. Although it had been a farm building of some kind, it was made into a residence. [*Top photo courtesy of Betty Thurne*]

JONATHAN KNIGHT HOUSE: Rev. Knight was born in 1760 in Cranston. He was a Private of Artillery in the Revolutionary War from March 1776 until January 1779. He served in several companies and spent nine months serving on the frigate *Providence*. Jonathan also served in the RI General Assembly. He died in 1842 in this house on Laten Knight Road which was then owned by his son, Sheldon. He is buried in the nearby Knight Lot. The top photo was taken around 1950 when the house was owned by Bryon Lawton. It remains a private home.

FISKEVILLE POST OFFICE: This building at 197 Main Street was the home of Lillian Salisbury, who was the former postmistress of the post office once housed there. Several generations of her family served in the same capacity. The post office serves more than one community and is now located across the street, having moved from Cranston to Scituate. Fiskeville was started by Dr. Caleb Fiske who settled in Scituate, near Cranston, in the late eighteenth century. He built a dam on the river and a cotton mill there in 1812. [*Top photo curtesy of Betty Thurne*]

FISKEVILLE TOWN HALL: The building at 287 Main Street has housed both the Fiskeville Town Hall and the Fiskeville Grange. The town hall was built in the hopes of the village becoming its own legal entity, but the village has remained split between Cranston and Scituate. The grange was active in supporting farmers for many years and was the birthplace of the Fiskeville Fair, held there in Cranston until it was moved across the street to Scituate. [*Top photo courtesy of Betty Thurne*]

FISKE FAMILY FUNERAL: The house at 467 Seven Mile Road was once owned by the Fiskes. In the early twentieth century, a funeral for a member of the Fiske family was being held in the parlor of the house when the floor began to give way. The mourners were rushed out of the house and Daniel Searle, a neighbor, and others went into the basement to shore up the floor with logs so that the funeral could continue. Annie King, granddaughter of William Warren Knight can be seen in the *circa* 1900 photo. The house has been well maintained as a residence. [*Top photo courtesy of Betty Thurne*]

HILLSIDE FARMS: Western Cranston had numerous dairy farms before many of them went out of business. This one on Phenix Avenue was in operation more than fifty years and was one of RI's largest independent dairies. In the 1980s, the 100 acres were made into a subdivision of houses. In May 1981, a nineteen-year-old pilot on the way to North Central State Airport in Smithfield had to land a Cessna 127 in one of the fields because of heavy fog. One of the milking barns on the other side of the street is now part of the building that houses the Word of Life Convent Church.

Acknowledgments

Unless otherwise noted, all of the vintage photographs at the top of the pages are the property of the Cranston Historical Society. Similarly, the modern photographs were all taken by one of the authors unless noted.

Besides the people identified as giving photographs, we would like to thank two men who also contributed to the production of this book. Jim Hall is the curator of the Cranston Historical Society and since 2011 has voluntarily devoted thousands of hours to cataloging all the society's photographs, artifacts and print materials and entering their descriptions into a museum software program. His work has made the authors' research and selection of photographs much easier. Mike Klitzner, also a member of the Cranston Historical Society, contributed to the acquisition of new photographs as well as provided the identification and background information of many sites depicted in the book.

All proceeds from this book will go to the Cranston Historical Society for its mission to preserve, protect and promote Cranston's history.

About the Authors

Sandra Moyer and Janet Cullen Ragno, two members of the Cranston Historical Society, have collaborated in compiling and describing photographs showing how the city of Cranston has changed through the years. They hope that people who remember Cranston from their youth, as well as younger people interested in what existed before them, will all enjoy the "then and now" photographs in this book. All the proceeds from sales of this book will be donated to the Cranston Historical Society to help in its mission to protect, preserve and promote this city's history.